DISNEY · PIXAR

MONSTERS
UNIVERSITY
THE ESSENTIAL GUIDE

WRITTEN BY GLENN DAKIN

CONTENTS

Disney · PIXAR

MONSTERS UNIVERSITY

THE ESSENTIAL GUIDE

INTRODUCTION

Welcome to Monsters University, the place where real monsters are made! If you're hoping to become a top Scarer at Monsters, Inc., then our School of Scaring is for you. Be warned: it isn't going to be easy. If you just aren't scary enough, we will be the first to let you know. For some, the dream of being a Scarer can quickly turn into a nightmare. But never fear! At this college, we offer plenty of courses for you to sink your fangs into. It's time to get swotting, find your scary feet, compete in the Scare Games and make some new friends. Remember that drool is a tool – now get scaring!

- Staff at Monsters University

 MIKE

Little Mike Wazowski has had one aim in life since he was six years old: to become a Scarer and work for Monsters, Inc. There is just one problem: Mike isn't that frightening. But he is a born trier and believes that hard work and study at Monsters University can make him the best there is.

SCHOOL DAYS

Never too popular as a kid, Mike was always the first one with his hand up in class, and often had to be partners with his teacher. When he arrives at university, he hopes those lonely days are behind him.

MONSTERS
UNIVERSITY

NAME: Mike Wazowski
SCARE SKILL: Brains and sharp wit

STUDENT

When he was just a school-monster, Mike went on a tour of Monsters, Inc. Taking a peep into the human realm had a big impact on him.

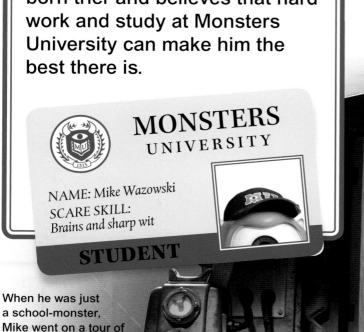

KNOW-IT-ALL

Mike knows every technique from Zombie Snarl to Ogre's Slump. However, when it comes to making people scream, Mike just doesn't have scary bones – no matter how many hours of late-night studying he puts in!

My lucky MU cap – no borrowing!

I've been waiting for this my whole life!

One eye is better than two. Well, Mum always says so.

Sometimes I think my fangs will never grow good 'n' crooked!

SCARE SCORE

5%

ROAR RECRUIT

Mike has plenty of skills to make up for the fact that he looks about as monstrous as a tennis ball. He is a quick learner and can bring out the best in those around him. Once he teams up with Sulley he becomes part of an unstoppable team.

TRUE OR FALSE?

Mike is a natural quitter.

FALSE – he never gives up!

# SULLEY

Big, blue and born to scare, Sulley is the kind of monster who stands out, even in a crowd of monsters. He is full of pranks and fun to be with – as long as you're not on the wrong end of one of his practical jokes.

MONSTERS
UNIVERSITY

NAME: James P. Sullivan
SCARE SKILL: Legendary roar

STUDENT

THE FRIGHT STUFF

No-one can out-scare this talented terror, who has the coolest roar on campus. Laid-back Sulley believes he knows everything there is to know about scaring. However, teaming up with Mike forces him to overcome his pride and shows him he still has a lot to learn.

Sulley is not big on note-taking – if he asks to borrow a pencil, he is more likely to pick his teeth with it.

SCARE PIG PRANK

Sulley enters Mike's life in a dramatic way when he climbs into his room and causes chaos with a stolen scare pig. Neither is impressed with the other from this first meeting – and they certainly don't want to be friends!

Curled horns make me extra scary!

You don't need to study scaring, you just do it!

SCARE SCORE

85%

HIGH HOPES

As the son of legendary Scarer Bill Sullivan, big things are expected of Sulley. Everyone treats him like a hero even before he has done anything to deserve it. He doubts he can live up to expectations, and secretly feels like a failure.

My soft blue fur hides the pure monster within.

TRUE OR FALSE?

Sulley and Mike become best friends straight away.

FALSE – they take an instant dislike to each other!

Girls go for cute purple spots. It's a Sullivan trade mark.

MONSTERS UNIVERSITY

This is the world-famous Monsters University, where "extraordinary" comes as standard. Thinking of enrolling? Then embark on a tour of this cool campus free of charge. If your future is knocking, come here – and open the door!

SCHOOL OF DOOR TECHNOLOGY

If other worlds intrigue you, try the Door Tech Lab. From here it is just a short step into the terrifying human world!

Engineering

Troll Bridge

COLLEGE ENTRANCE

Hopes and dreams begin here, as freshmen embark on a new life the instant they step off the bus.

Scream Can Design

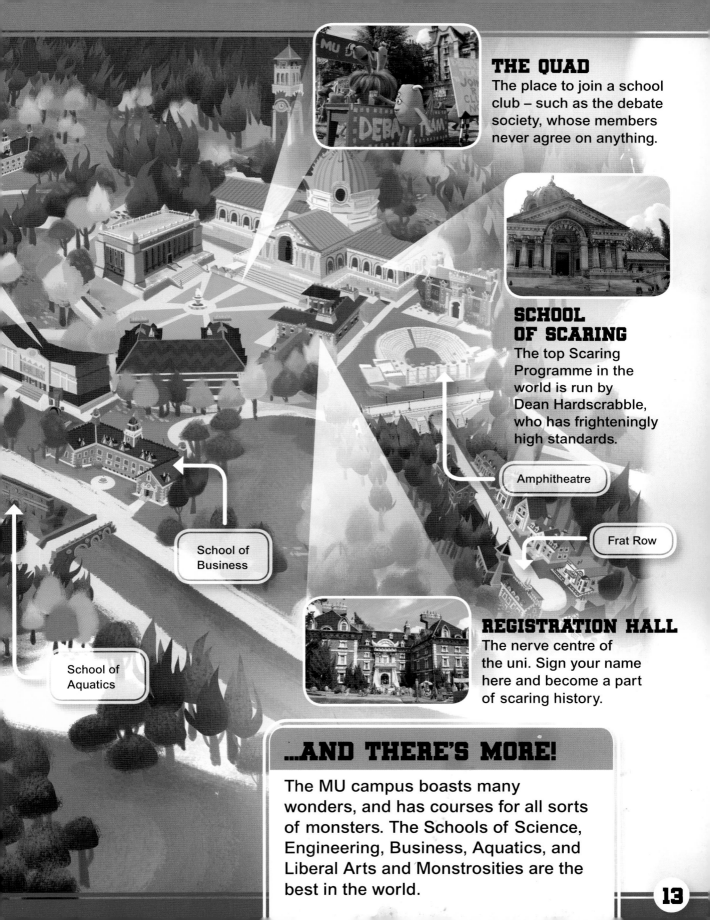

THE QUAD

The place to join a school club – such as the debate society, whose members never agree on anything.

SCHOOL OF SCARING

The top Scaring Programme in the world is run by Dean Hardscrabble, who has frighteningly high standards.

Amphitheatre

Frat Row

School of Business

School of Aquatics

REGISTRATION HALL

The nerve centre of the uni. Sign your name here and become a part of scaring history.

...AND THERE'S MORE!

The MU campus boasts many wonders, and has courses for all sorts of monsters. The Schools of Science, Engineering, Business, Aquatics, and Liberal Arts and Monstrosities are the best in the world.

Settling in

Every student has a lot to do when they arrive at Monsters University – it's just that some are more organised than others. Mike is so determined to become a great Scarer that he has every step of the way marked out on a checklist!

3. Take the tour
Fay the tour guide takes the freshmen around the hallowed halls of MU. Highlights include the door lab, the School of Scaring and the equally frightening recycled food in the cafeteria.

2. Get student card
The next stop is getting your photo taken for your student card. Mike is so thrilled to get his that he doesn't notice he barely makes it into the picture!

1. Get registered
The Smile Squad are ready to welcome all new students. Kay the R.A. (Resident Assistant) gives out welcome packs – and heaps of sheer enthusiasm.

4. Move in to dorm

Ray the R.A. gives Mike the key to his room — number 319. He is sharing with Randy Boggs — another Scaring student. Maybe they'll be best pals for life!

5. Meet roommate

Even making new friends is carefully timetabled by Mike. He hopes his new pal Randy will help test him with course work, and never try to drag him out partying!

Mike's list

No student could be better prepared for university than Mike. His tight schedule even includes the right moment to hang up his posters. The last items on his list may prove harder to achieve — things like "Ace my classes" and "Become the greatest Scarer ever" are easier planned than done!

RANDY

This snaky scaring student has everything it takes to be properly petrifying – but he is too sweet-natured at first to realise that. Shy and nervous, Randy admires his roommate Mike for his great confidence and drive.

MONSTERS UNIVERSITY

NAME:
Randall "Randy" Boggs
SCARE SKILL: Blending ability

STUDENT

Randy appears in shadow when he first meets Mike, giving out a falsely sinister first impression.

RANDY'S TRICK

Randy has a surprise for his new roomie – a habit of camouflaging that he doesn't quite know how to control. Mike has just one tip – take off the glasses – they kind of spoil the effect.

DID YOU KNOW?

Randy and Sulley go head-to-head in the Scare Games final. It seems those two monsters are destined to be always competing.

I'm so nervous!

Geeky purple glasses make me look cute.

"BE MY PAL"

On the night of a big fraternity party, Mike stays in to study. Eager-to-please Randy heads out with a tray of cupcakes, keen to do what he does best – blend in.

These silly scales are always disappearing into the background on me!

Multiple limbs are handy when the professor asks for "hands up!"

TOP TALENT

At first unsure that he has the abilities to cut it as a Scarer, Randy is surprised to be invited to join the top fraternity, Roar Omega Roar (ROR). Clearly they see potential in him – or maybe they just love that they can't see him at all!

SCARE SCORE

84%

FAVOURITE CAP

Mike's most precious possession is the Monsters University baseball cap he was given by a Monsters, Inc. Scarer on a school field trip. A little faded and frayed, it reminds him of the hopes and dreams he's treasured since he was a kid.

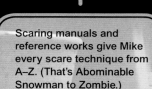

Scaring manuals and reference works give Mike every scare technique from A–Z. (That's Abominable Snowman to Zombie.)

MIKE'S ROOM

Every scaring-obsessed monster needs a cosy place he can go back to in the evening and obsess about scaring some more. Mike is quick to turn the room he shares with Randy into the perfect study, from where he can mastermind his great career.

PETRIFYING POSTERS

Mike has only one real love – scaring. Every poster, book and magazine he owns is on this terrifying topic. He is sure his roommate Randy will find his pictures as inspiring as he does!

RANDY'S SPACE

Eagle-eyed observers will note that the right-hand side of the room is not covered in scaring memorabilia. This is Randy's part of the room, and he prefers to keep things normal – even tasteful – so as not to stand out from the crowd too much.

Randy takes great inspiration from this poster. He is looking out for the "winds of change" in his life.

WINDS OF CHANGE
Shhh. Do you hear that?

Archie the Scare Pig – the mascot for rival school, Fear Tech – was accidentally let loose in Mike's room after Sulley stole it to impress the ROR fraternity.

TEDDY SCARE

Just like him, Mike's favourite teddy, "Little Mikey," has only the one eye. Mike couldn't resist bringing this beloved "bear" to university with him.

SCHOOL OF SCARING

At the heart of Monsters University is the School of Scaring – a grand chamber filled with statues of the great Scarers who have taught there. Hundreds of students participate in Professor Knight's classes every year, but only a few will ever pass its ultimate tests.

Shifty eyes, on the lookout for problem students.

TOUCHING TRADITION

As the bells of the university ring out across the campus, the eager students rush to class. Everyone touches the statue as they pass by – it is an old school tradition, bringing much-needed luck!

Sensible shirt and tie reflect traditional approach.

"I expect big things of you..."
– Professor Knight

If the students thought Professor Knight was formidable, they are in for a bigger scare when Dean Hardscrabble swoops down to pay them a visit. The fresh-faced new students may be training to be Scarers, but, for now, they are the ones being scared!

PROFESSOR KNIGHT
Teaching the introductory course at MU, Scaring 101, is old-school tough guy, Professor Derek Knight. He is quick to tell the new students that though they may have been the scariest monster in their own little town, they are in the big league now. He wants them to impress him – and he does not scare easily!

ROARING SUCCESS
One of the many lessons in Scaring 101 is how to perform the perfect roar. This is a subject in which Sulley needs no coaching! However, as Professor Knight points out, one frightening face does not a monster make.

DEAN HARDSCRABBLE

A living legend, this proud professor casts a long shadow over Monsters University. Dean Hardscrabble believes that monsters only exist to scare, and without that power they are nobody. Having decided that Mike isn't scary, she considers him finished on the Scaring Programme.

MONSTERS
UNIVERSITY

NAME: *Abigail Hardscrabble*
SCARE SKILL: *All-rounder*

STAFF

There is nothing about Dean Hardscrabble that isn't scary. On the first day of term, she makes an appearance that even alarms Professor Knight!

INSPIRING LEADER

When asked to say a few words of inspiration on the first day of class, Dean Hardscrabble terrifies them all by revealing that if they don't pass their first exam, they are out of the Scaring Programme forever.

DID YOU KNOW?

Hardscrabble founded the Scare Games when she was a student, and won them four years in a row!

RECORD HOLDER

The dean's most precious possession is the can that contains her record-breaking scream. This one souvenir of her great career is accidentally wrecked by Mike and Sulley.

GAMES MASTER

One of Hardscrabble's many duties is to open the Scare Games. When the expelled Mike and Sulley enter, she reluctantly agrees that if their team can win the games, they will all be allowed into the Scaring Programme. Of course, she believes they have no chance.

> Scariness is the true measure of a monster.

Always fold your wings away neatly when not in use.

ALWAYS RIGHT

This seasoned Scarer has shrewd instincts, which she trusts completely. Once she has decided that someone isn't scary, she never changes her mind. Being challenged by Mike and Sulley is a whole new experience for her, and one she treats with utter scorn.

Well-manicured claws are more hygienic, and horrific.

Even the way you walk can be scary — particularly with multiple, skittering legs.

23

SULLEY VS MIKE

Every student has a different outlook on university life. Let's check out the feedback that two typical college freshmen gave on an MU questionnaire!

NAME: JAMES SULLIVAN

What is your attitude towards the following...

1. Class?

A great place to get laughs. It's good to arrive late – that way you grab everyone's attention. Teachers love to have a famous Sullivan in their group, so it's kind of plain sailing.

2. Your first day?

Studying can wait! The first day is all about pulling a crazy stunt to impress the top fraternity, ROR. I stole Fear Tech's mascot – beat that!

3. Joining a fraternity?

Joining a group is really important – so you can spend most of the first term partying. I think that's what everyone expects of you, and I don't aim to disappoint.

4. Exams?

They gave me a "C-minus" in my test! No Sullivan has ever rated that low. Maybe there IS something to this studying stuff. What? Wazowski got an "A-plus"? How could that happen?

What is your attitude towards the following...

1. Class?

An ace student is most at home when fielding tough questions in a highly competitive classroom situation! Get your hand up first and learn all the key answers by heart.

2. Spare time?

Are you kidding me? This is a trick question, right? A future Scarer has no free time when he's at MU. He gets his head down and he studies 24/7. Maybe more.

3. Practice?

Nothing beats it! A mirror isn't for personal grooming, it's for practising scary faces. Snarling never gets old.

4. Exams?

Every course has an easy part, and I guess exams are it. I mean, I can list 100 phobias before breakfast! I knew I was going to get an "A-plus" in my exam, but a certain big blue guy seems a little shaken...

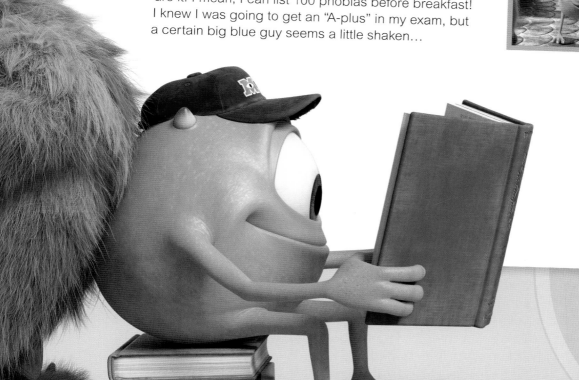

JOHNNY WORTHINGTON

Top scare student and president of the popular Roar Omega Roar fraternity, Johnny is the monster who seems to have everything. With brains as well as brawn, he rules the roost on campus and decides who is in the "in-crowd" and who gets left behind.

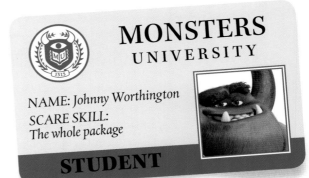

MONSTERS
UNIVERSITY

NAME: *Johnny Worthington*
SCARE SKILL:
The whole package

STUDENT

TRUE OR FALSE?

Johnny is a true friend to Sulley.

FALSE – he only likes him when he thinks he has top Scarer potential.

Johnny and the ROR gang are quick to welcome Sulley into their ranks after he causes chaos at the fraternity party by stealing Fear Tech's mascot.

TEAM ROR

Johnny and his pals at ROR are all from rich, important families. They are cool, easy-going guys – while everything is going their way. But they turn nasty really quickly if someone tries to outdo them.

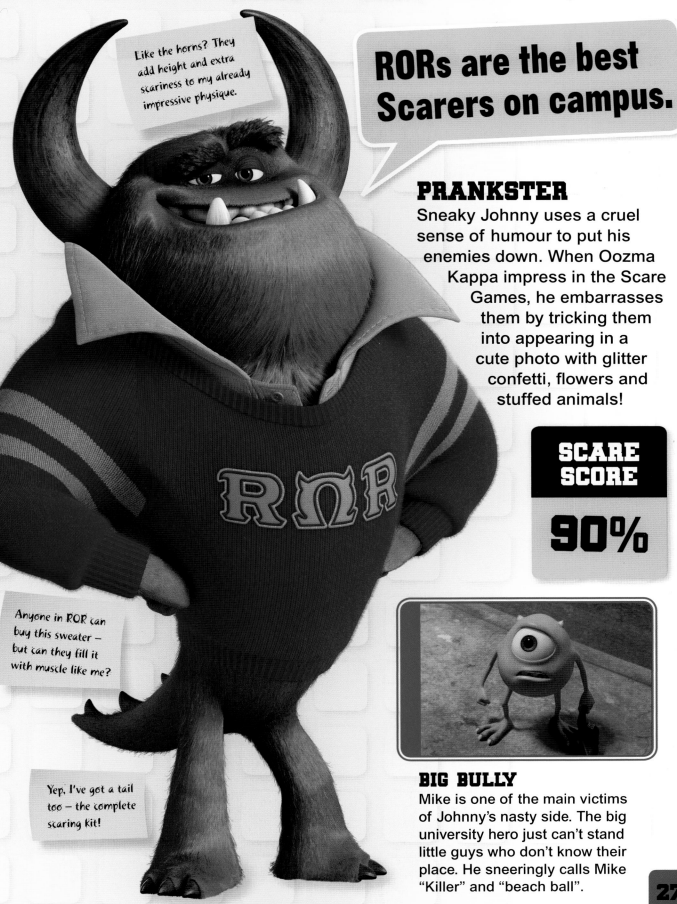

Like the horns? They add height and extra scariness to my already impressive physique.

RORs are the best Scarers on campus.

PRANKSTER

Sneaky Johnny uses a cruel sense of humour to put his enemies down. When Oozma Kappa impress in the Scare Games, he embarrasses them by tricking them into appearing in a cute photo with glitter confetti, flowers and stuffed animals!

SCARE SCORE

90%

Anyone in ROR can buy this sweater – but can they fill it with muscle like me?

Yep, I've got a tail too – the complete scaring kit!

BIG BULLY

Mike is one of the main victims of Johnny's nasty side. The big university hero just can't stand little guys who don't know their place. He sneeringly calls Mike "Killer" and "beach ball".

SCARE FINAL

There is one day that stands out among all others for scare students at MU – the day of their final scare exam. Professor Knight and Dean Hardscrabble are there to judge a very anxious crop of young hopefuls.

This day has been marked on Mike's calendar since the beginning of term. After all his swotting, surely nothing can go wrong now?

SCARE SIMULATOR

Every student must face their turn in the scare simulator: a recreation of a human bedroom, containing a working model of a child. Here, a monster's abilities to assess that child's fears and then scare accordingly are measured under controlled conditions.

Offstage, Professor Knight summons students one by one to perform their scare.

RED LETTER DAY

Even on exam day, Mike and Sulley can't ignore their rivalry. Inside the School of Scaring, they argue and accidentally break Hardscrabble's prized scream can. Ominously, the dean herself then takes over their exam...

CRACKLE AND HOLLER

The dean asks Mike to provide the right scare to terrify a five-year-old girl on a farm in Kansas, who is scared of lightning. Mike knows the right approach, but the frosty dean doesn't even let him get his scream out. She has made up her mind.

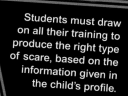

Students must draw on all their training to produce the right type of scare, based on the information given in the child's profile.

EXPELLED

The exam ends with a shocking outcome: both Mike and Sulley are thrown off the Scaring Programme. Hardscrabble believes that Mike is just not scary, and that Sulley's reckless, unthinking scares could cause the end of monster civilisation!

"I've seen enough."
– Dean Hardscrabble

LET THE GAMES BEGIN!

The whole campus is buzzing as teams gather for the kick-off of the annual Greek Scare Games! This year a bit more drama has been added to the occasion, as Dean Hardscrabble herself is challenged by a little green monster who just won't give up on his dreams…

"May the best monsters win!"
– Dean Hardscrabble

COUNCIL RULES
Anyone wanting to take part in the games must sign up for the event with the Greek Council. The Council President is a stickler for rules: to enter you must be in a team of six – and you can't count a two-headed monster as two team members!

SECOND CHANCES
When Mike and Sulley are expelled, they are relegated to the Scream Can Design Programme. For a cool creature like Sulley to end up in such a lowly position really is monstrous. He thinks his fate is sealed – until he learns that his annoying green rival has found a way back into the Scaring Programme…

A DEAL WITH THE DEAN

Mike manages to cut a deal with Dean Hardscrabble: if his team can win the Scare Games, it will prove that she is wrong about him not being scary, and they will all be allowed onto the Scaring Programme. She agrees – on condition that failure will result in him leaving MU forever!

SULLEY STEPS IN

To enter the games, Mike teams up with the least scary fraternity of all – Oozma Kappa – but they are still one member short. Just when it looks as if Mike will fail before he begins, Sulley shows up. Sulley realises Mike's deal with the dean is his ticket back to the Scaring Programme too – and a famous duo is born!

OOZMA KAPPA

Not every fraternity can be at the top of the popularity charts. Oozma Kappa (OK) is a society for monsters who have failed to impress and been cut from the Scaring Programme. Although these guys are kind and warm-hearted, it is just possible that they are a lot scarier than they realise.

If you like our sweater, I'm sure Squishy's mum will knit you one!

MUM KNOWS BEST

The secret weapon of the OKs is Squishy's proud mum. Ms Squibbles provides their house, outfits, cookies and getaway car.

Terri and Terry Perry

Art

I may actually be asleep in this picture — I'm just dreaming I'm awake!

SACRED OATH

To join Oozma Kappa, Mike and Sulley have to swear to be loyal, in the face of unending pain – or at least a whack with a paddle!

DID YOU KNOW?

The rules of the Scare Games say that fraternities must win as a unit. Mike and Sulley race ahead in the first challenge, but their whole team must cross the line in order to finish!

GET-ALONG GANG

Once entered for the Scare Games, the OKs think it might be useful to list their strengths. Terri and Terry claim they're master magicians, and noisy Don thinks he could sneak up on a mouse in a pillow factory. Mike tells them to bury these instincts deep down and focus on scaring – his way!

Sulley

For a top scaring asset, grow a moustache that looks like a bat!

Don Carlton

Scott Squibbles (aka Squishy)

Mike

33

OOZMA KAPPA HQ

This quaint suburban villa is home to the Oozma Kappa fraternity. It may not be the coolest fraternity house on campus, but it is certainly the cosiest, and is owned by Squishy's kind-hearted mum. If you're a little different from the crowd, or just not wanted anywhere else, you'll always be welcome here.

A downstairs light is left on all night because Squishy is scared of the dark.

PARTY CENTRAL

The living room is where all the fun will happen – if the OKs ever get their disco ball fixed and if Squishy's mum says he is allowed to stay up late. There is always warm cocoa and sometimes the extreme craziness of building a cushion fort.

Flowers, chintz curtains and patterned wallpaper are not at all scary, but reflect Ms Squibbles's quaint style.

New members are placed in this top bedroom, and pranked by having the lights turned off in a phoney power cut.

BUNK BUDDIES

Mike and Sulley share this tiny room in their new house. The cramped quarters mean they get to know each other fast – especially their weird habits. For a start, Sulley sheds fur like it's going out of fashion.

HOME SWEET HOME

Ms Squibbles's home provides a safe haven for each and every member of Oozma Kappa. An eclectic bunch, and rejected by the "cool" kids on campus, they are looking for a new direction in life, and are keen to support each other in any way that they can.

Below here is the basement where the initiation ceremony takes place.

BELOW STAIRS

Down in the basement is where Squishy likes to hold the secret welcome ritual for new members. It is supposed to be an impressive ceremony, but is ruined when his mum comes wandering down to do her laundry!

SQUISHY

Childlike and cheerful, this nervous 19-year-old is the heart and soul of the Oozma Kappa gang. Squishy loves to make new members welcome, and if there is anything he can't personally provide then his mum is happy to step in.

MONSTERS
UNIVERSITY

NAME: Scott "Squishy" Squibbles
SCARE SKILL: Sneaking

STUDENT

THE KAPPA CAP

He may lack confidence in himself, but Squishy is very proud of his fraternity. He likes to perform the oath of allegiance and hand over an OK cap to all new members.

SCARE SCORE

75%

This is just one of many OK sweaters my mum has knitted for me.

Squishy rarely raises his voice, but he does get agitated when his mum is slow to drive off after their trip to Monsters, Inc. Ms Squibbles won't be rushed – she needs to check that all seat-belts have been fastened, and then wants to offer everyone a piece of gum!

TRUE OR FALSE?

Squishy is rough, tough and independent.

FALSE – he is happy to be a mummy's boy.

I've never stayed up this late in my life!

Having five eyes means I can always see more than one point of view!

SULLEY FAN

Squishy is thrilled to have some real scary monsters in the gang – the OKs are sure to do well in the Scare Games with Mike and Sulley on board. He is particularly impressed that Sulley's hand is as big as his face!

GAMES HERO

Fading into the background is something this polite little monster has a natural gift for. Not being noticed isn't always an advantage, but it sure comes in handy in the "Avoid the Parent" Scare Games event, when Squishy evades the librarian and takes the flag for his team!

My soft feet are perfect for creeping up on people.

DON CARLTON

This mild-mannered monster is the president of the OKs. Don learned a lot from his early years as a salesman – mainly that he wasn't wanted any more! Now he has enrolled at MU as a mature student, seeking a new start.

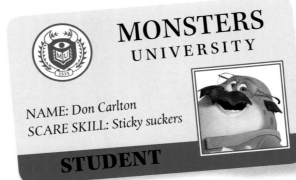

MONSTERS
UNIVERSITY

NAME: *Don Carlton*
SCARE SKILL: *Sticky suckers*

STUDENT

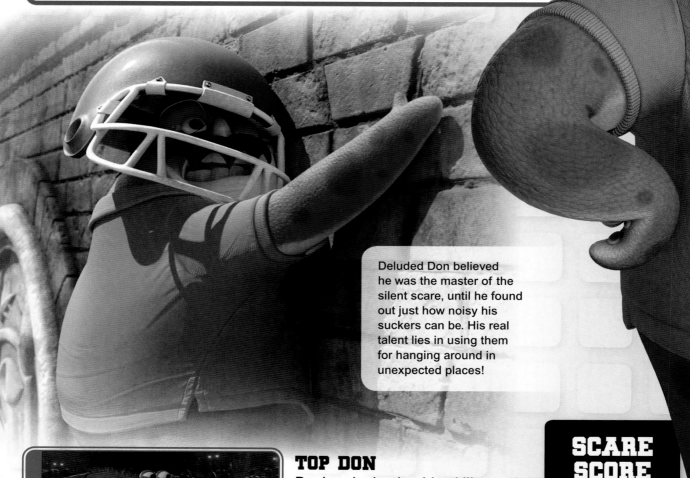

Deluded Don believed he was the master of the silent scare, until he found out just how noisy his suckers can be. His real talent lies in using them for hanging around in unexpected places!

TOP DON

Don's calm leadership skills shine when the OKs make it to the Scare Games final. He steps out first in the head-to-head against ROR and earns a high score in the simulator – putting OK in the lead!

SCARE SCORE

75%

Anything you need, you just give a big holleroony!

I'm Don Carlton from Sales — it says so on my card.

DON CARLTON
SALES

My super suckers make a not-so-scary noise when I get sweaty.

DID YOU KNOW?

One habit the ex-salesman can't quit is his fondness for handing out business cards. After his successes in the Scare Games, his cards now read "Scarer" rather than "Sales".

LIVING THE DREAM

Don has a permanently positive outlook on life: When he was let go by his sales company, he refused to throw a pity party and give up! Now he is learning about computers and getting reschooled in scaring. With Mike helping him develop his skills, Don knows it is never too late to go after your dreams.

TERRI & TERRY

They say that two heads are better than one, but this split personality isn't always so sure! One thing the Oozma Kappa brothers Terri and Terry Perry do share is a love of bickering – and a dream of becoming Scarers.

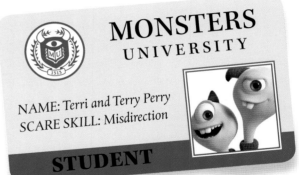

MONSTERS
UNIVERSITY

NAME: Terri and Terry Perry
SCARE SKILL: Misdirection

STUDENT

Terri and Terry plan a disco ball welcome for new members Mike and Sulley. When it crashes straight to the floor, they confess they've never had a real party!

PARTY MONSTERS

Terri and Terry have a gift for crazy dance routines, but can't always agree on when or where to perform them. The failed routine usually ends with an argument and public humiliation.

TRUE OR FALSE?

A two-headed monster only counts as one team member in the Scare Games.

TRUE! – despite their twin heads, Terri and Terry add up to only one member of OK.

HEAD START

The brothers are given a boost when they visit Monsters, Inc. Their two-headed issues don't seem so bad when they spot a *three*-headed Scarer on a scare floor!

My uni-horn is cooler than Terry's old-school pairing.

You should wake up embarrassed!

Our extra arms are useful for magic tricks. (We store the cards up our sleeves!)

My favourite fizzy drink is Blort! Big bro prefers tea in china cups. Weirdo.

DOUBLE TROUBLE

Despite being physically inseparable, these brothers have very different personalities. "Terry with a 'y'" is older by several seconds, and sees himself as the wise old cynic of the duo. "Terri with an 'i'" is the naïve, young kid, who often gets put in his place. But they can work together, and their misdirection skills are invaluable in helping to confuse the librarian in the second Scare Games challenge.

A creature of mystery, this new age philosophy student is a loyal member of Oozma Kappa. In a time of crisis, he can always be relied upon – to do something unexpected and bizarre.

DREAM KEEPER

One of Art's many kooky habits is keeping a dream journal. It is a practice he thinks everyone should join in with, and he even gives Mike and Sulley books for them to do it in.

MONSTERS
UNIVERSITY

NAME: Art
SCARE SKILL:
Extreme weirdness

STUDENT

SCARE SCORE

70%

Standing upside-down makes me look more intelligent, don't you think?

MEDITATION GURU

Art is scared of working-out because he claims he is frightened of getting too big. He prefers meditation and yoga to exercise – as long as he can do it in his own unique way.

MYSTERY MONSTER

Prone to dropping baffling remarks about his past and hobbies, Art claims to have an extra toe (not on him, of course). He is also fond of sewer 14, which he says is his favourite of all the sewers on campus.

My purple fuzz keeps wrecking Squishy's mum's vacuum cleaner.

When nearly caught on the roof of Monsters, Inc., Art shocks his pals by confessing that he was once in prison!

DID YOU KNOW?

Art has a weird curiosity about everything – including touching the highly toxic glow urchins he has been told to avoid in the first Scare Games event.

These gappy teeth are too regular to be scary!

Unleash the beast!

START HERE!

ARE YOU NATURALLY SCARY?

YES → IS BEING SCARY ALL ABOUT HAVING THE LOUDEST ROAR?

WHAT KIND OF SCARER ARE YOU?

Ever wondered how you would turn out if you enrolled at Monsters University? It isn't just about how hard you study – every detail of your personality affects the outcome! Try our quick quiz to find out – but choose your answers carefully, because the dean might be watching!

NOT SURE

NO

DO YOU EVEN WANT TO BE A SCARER?

← NO ← ARE YOU PREPARED TO GIVE YOUR ALL AND NEVER GIVE UP, EVEN IN THE FACE OF ADVERSITY?

NO

YES

YES

WHY ARE YOU DOING THIS QUIZ? TRY SCREAM CAN DESIGN!

ARE YOU A NATURAL TEAM LEADER?

YES ➡️

IS BEING THE BEST MORE IMPORTANT THAN HAVING FRIENDS?

➡️ **NO**

SULLEY

Like Sulley, you could be a great Scarer! But use your head as well as your howl, and learn to look before you creep.

NO ➡️

YES ➡️

JOHNNY

You are a truly horrible monster! Are you already a member of ROR? You'd fit right in!

YES ➡️

DO YOU KNOW THE DIFFERENCE BETWEEN SCARING TECHNIQUES LIKE ZOMBIE SNARL AND OGRE'S SLUMP?

➡️ **YES**

MIKE

You turned out like Mike. You know your stuff, and are determined to succeed, no matter what. How about trying for a job at Monsters, Inc.?

NO ➡️

SQUISHY

You are just like Squishy – scary, but soft-hearted. You are a friendly monster, but with cool hidden abilities!

 # ROR

Winners of the Scare Games for the last three years in a row, Roar Omega Roar is the oldest fraternity on campus. Its members all went to the best public schools – not that they ever learned much about being nice to those less privileged!

LAP OF LUXURY

Frat Row on campus is where many fraternity houses can be found. The ROR house looks like a luxury hotel and is where ROR proudly store all their trophies.

The four-armed limited edition sweater is the most stylish, no?

Chip Goff

Javier Rios

THE IN CROWD?

ROR consider themselves the coolest fraternity, but they are far from the nicest. This gang stays together through a shared big-headedness, rather than true friendship. Reaching the final of the Scare Games was always a given for them. But going up against the uncool fraternity, Oozma Kappa, was not!

Chet Alexander

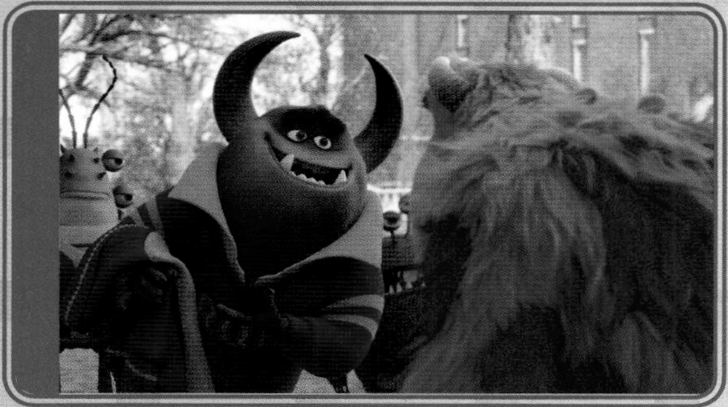

TOUGH AT THE TOP

Being a member of ROR isn't guaranteed for life – one sign of weakness and you risk being thrown out. Johnny takes Sulley's ROR jacket away from him when he looks likely to flunk his final exam.

DID YOU KNOW?

The legendary Scarer, Earl "The Terror" Thompson, is a former ROR. He has a top job at Monsters, Inc.

ROR members are all expert at posing for group portraits. We have them taken a lot.

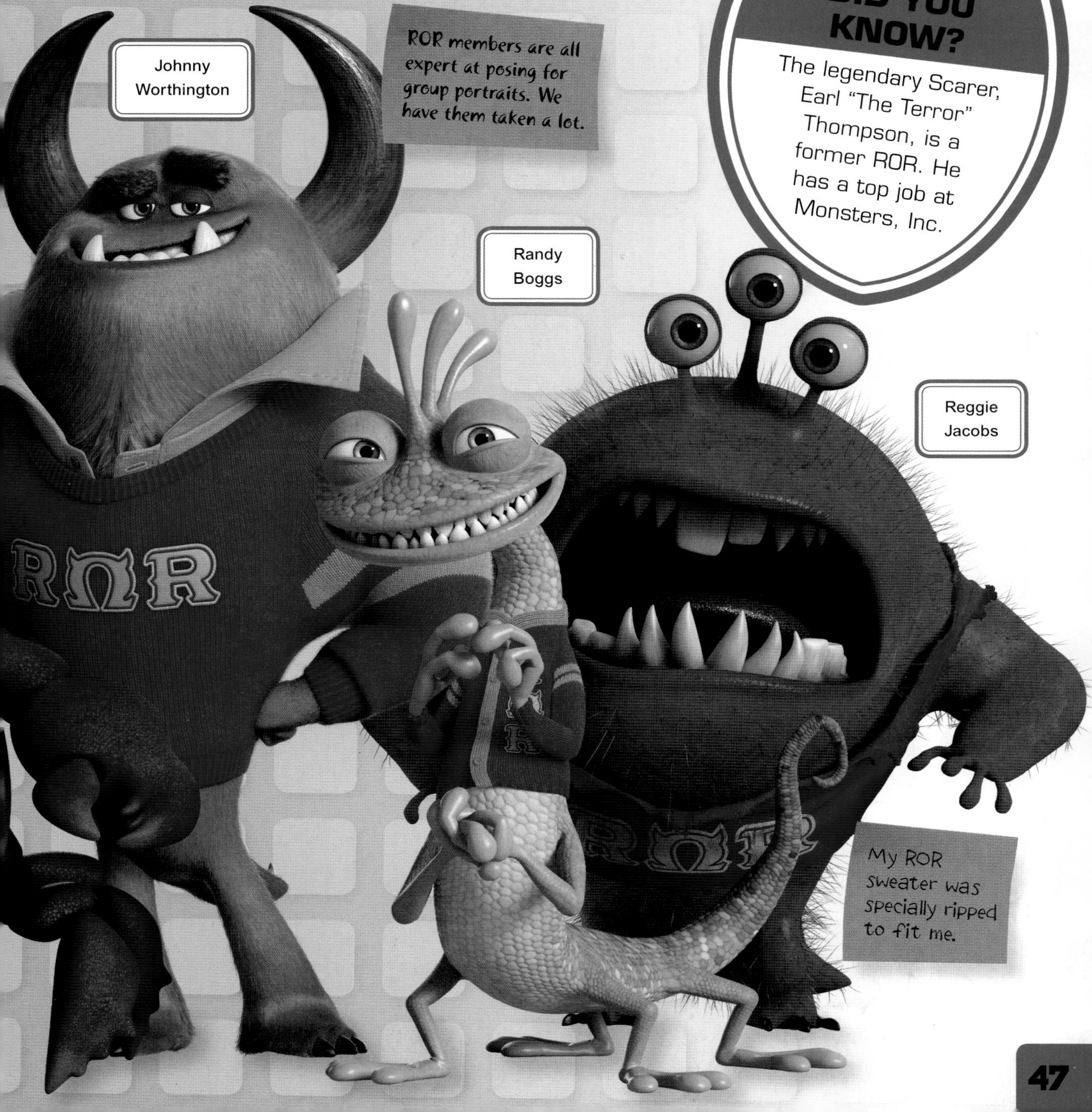

Johnny Worthington
Randy Boggs
Reggie Jacobs
ROR

My ROR sweater was specially ripped to fit me.

FIELD TRIP

When the Oozma Kappa fraternity are beginning to doubt they have the fright stuff to become real Scarers, Mike decides to take them on a little field trip to Monsters, Inc. It's time they all took a look at life in the big leagues…

An awesome sight during the day, the Monsters, Inc. factory is just that bit more intimidating by night.

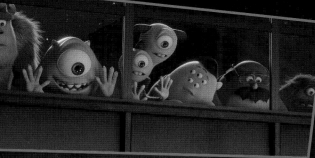

SNEAKY PEEK

Taking to the roof, the gang get a perfect view of a scare floor. Here they can see the best Scarers in the business at work, and get inspired – as long as they don't get caught!

CUTTING IN

If there is no official entrance to the factory for late-night callers, then Mike is quite happy to make one, with a handy pair of wire cutters. Nothing is going to keep him from his favourite place in all the world – and a certain lesson he wants to teach his friends.

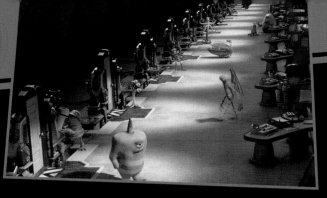

SCARING MASTERCLASS

Peering down at some world-famous Scarers, Mike asks his friends to spot what they all have in common. The answer is… nothing! Mike proves to his pals that Scarers succeed by using their differences to their advantage.

"There's no ONE type of Scarer."
– Mike

QUICK GETAWAY

When it is time to make a swift exit, the panicked OKs realise that their best bet for avoiding capture is hitching a ride on Sulley. Their big blue buddy begins to show some true team spirit as he helps them all flee the guards.

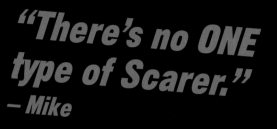

JOX

The JOX (Jaws Theta Chi fraternity) are the snarliest students on campus, but they are the kind of muscle-brained monsters who prove that big doesn't always mean scary. Ultra-competitive, these guys are happy to cheat if it means getting results.

You are Jaws Theta Chi material, freshmen!

RED-HANDED

The JOX president, Big Red, initially wanted Sulley for his fraternity, but lost out to ROR. He then got his team disqualified for wearing illegal protective gel in the Toxicity Challenge. He claims it was just moisturiser!

Check out the classy JOX logo on my stripe!

MOUTHY MOB

The JOX hate losing, and they also hate losers. They're a flash crowd who like to show off their tacky yellow-and-red letterman jackets. What they lack in brains, they make up for with brawn – or so they hope.

A five-gallon protein shake a day keeps me in shape!

Omar Harris

George Sanderson

Percy Boleslaw

Dirk Pratt

Roy "Big Red" O'Growlahan

Baboso Goretega

EEK

The EEKs (Slugma Slugma Kappa) are a super-athletic sorority, obsessed with training and running scare-drills. If you join this team, say goodbye to your sofa, as loafing around is not on the agenda.

SHOCK EXIT

The EEKs start the Scare Games with a good third position in the Toxicity Challenge, but make a surprise early exit in round two, when the librarian knocks down their monster pyramid! The purple princesses simply can't believe they are squeezed out by the OKs.

Don't dare confuse us with those stupid pink PNKs — we're much scarier!

What do you mean, "how do you see through all your hair?" My eyes are in my tail!

In this sorority, if you don't like purple or sweatbands, keep it to yourself!

Carla Delgado

Violet Steslicki

Donna Soohoo

Brynn Larson

Debbie Gabler

Maria Garcia

PNK

Don't be fooled by the cute looks of this pretty-in-pink crowd – the sweet smiles of the PNK (Python Nu Kappa) sorority hide the cold hearts of the meanest monsters in MU. Instead of futures in fashion, these monsters are hoping for careers in crematoriums.

DID YOU KNOW?

You wouldn't want to meet these girls at night – all of the PNKs have eyes that light up in the dark. One of the gang has heat-ray vision, but don't look too close to find out which one!

We're gonna rip you to pieces!

LETHAL LOOKS

Although they go to great lengths to look like each other, this creepy clique get annoyed when people can't tell them apart. Boys beware – a date with a PNK will usually end up in tears – and it won't be the girl doing the crying!

Heather Olson

Ignore my cute pose – I'm actually practising a new cheerleading move: "Jump and Twirl Attack".

Our lip colours are natural pigments. We wake up looking like this!

Britney Davis

Carrie Williams

Taylor Holbrook

Crystal Du Bois

Naomi Jackson

Our legwarmers and skirts are really naturally growing fur.

52

FAMOUS ALUMNI
Dean Hardscrabble herself used to be a member of HSS. However, when presiding over the Scare Games she does, of course, have to remain impartial.

HSS

If you enjoy wearing black and you like body piercings, HSS (Eta Hiss Hiss), led by the fiercely frightening Rosie Levin, is the sorority for you. Don't apply if you are merely slightly scary – this is a sisterhood for the deeply, deeply terrifying.

MONSTER MUSIC
One of the truly scary things about this current crop of HSS members is their taste in music. They perform together as an award-winning a cappella singing group.

My blue skin secretes an inky goo that I use in my hobby – tattooing!

Like my earrings? I get a new one every time we win an event – or when I make a grown man cry!

My punk hair spikes turn into stinging whips when I get my scare on.

Nancy Kim

Sonia Lewis

Susan Jensen

Rosie Levin

Nadya Petrov

Rhonda Boyd

SCARE GAMES NEWS!

There is no bigger story on campus than the drama of the Scare Games. Here's how the student paper tells the tales of ROR, JOX, EEK, PNK, HSS and OK, and their last-gasp wins, dire defeats and epic exits!

JOX JOLTED BY JUDGES

The JOX thought their fearsome line-up would bring them victory – not shame!

A shock disqualification got these games off to a sensational start! As all monsters know, there is nothing more toxic than a human child. The Toxicity Challenge is designed to test the teams' ability to avoid this peril – by sending them through a sewer-load of toxic urchins. As expected, ROR roared to victory, closely followed by JOX.

The OKs, finishing last, were all set to leave the contest when the judges spotted that the JOX had used illegal protective gel! It was no joke for JOX leade Big Red as the whole team was disqualified and the OK were okayed to continue! Dean Hardscrabble looked stunned – she was heard to say that the OKs' luck is sure to run out shortly!

EEKs in LiBRARY Exit

There was no call for silence in the "Avoid the Parent" event, as the OKs celebrated booking a place in the next round. The aim of this game is to capture your flag without disturbing the librarian, just as monsters have to avoid the parents in their trips to the human world. The EEKs tried to reach their flag by building a pyramid – only to be toppled by a tentacle. In a truly stunning tactic, never seen before in this event, the OKs gave up on being silent and distracted the librarian with a mad and noisy display! There was no fine for their weird method – the only rule here is don't get caught!

The normally-upbeat EEKs may need a few days to recover from their defeat.

PNK MAZE MIX-UP

The PNKs love to gossip, but probably didn't have their own defeat in mind as a talking point.

It was a day to be a-maze-d as the usually perfect PNKs went astray. The object of "Don't Scare the Teen" is to pass through the maze, scare the human child pop-ups and avoid the teen pop-ups. The crowd watched with excitement as the RORs raced to victory – then gasped in astonishment as the OKs emerged in second place!

The much-fancied (by themselves) PNKs had to accept the dreary reality of defeat. Oozma Kappa were delighted not only to get through, but to discover they are also picking up a lot of fans along the way. Well, everyone loves an underdog – apart from Dean Hardscrabble!

HSS-TORIC DRAMA

The Scare Games were shaken to the core today, when the hideous HSS sisters were swiftly spotted and thrown out of the "Hide and Sneak" event. Team members opted for traditional hiding places – behind the curtains and under the bed – leading to a quick discovery and dismissal by the referee. That surprise package, the OKs, were more original, with the fluffy Sullivan disguising himself as a luxurious rug. Beach-ball shaped Mike Wazowski hid behind a convenient globe! Proving they are more than just okay, the OKs will now make a historic first-ever appearance in the final. Of course, they stand no chance against the mighty RORs... Hey, Johnny told us to write that!

The gothic HSS sisters would still look gloomy even if they'd been announced champions!

 +  = FINAL

SCARE GAMES FINAL

Against all the odds, the OKs have made it to the final event of the Scare Games – the "Simulated Scare". The Scare Games have been full of surprises, and are about to have a sensational ending – but not in a way that anyone could have predicted. At the last minute, Sulley decides to give Mike a helping hand....

TEAM TACTICS

Mike had planned to go first in the final, but Sulley has other ideas. He says that as Mike started this thing, it is only right he should finish it. The other members agree, with Squishy urging him to finish strong. None of them suspect that Sulley has a sneaky trick up his sleeve....

The Scare Games trophy is abandoned by OK when they discover Sulley's treachery.

SQUISHY SMASHES IT

Squishy may not pack much of a roar, but he has a super-scary habit of creeping up unnoticed. The simulator kid lets out a big scream when Squishy pops up right by his bed. Mike's training has paid off – the OKs are now really scary!

TERRIBLE TRUTH

Mike's roof-raising scare means the OKs win the Scare Games, but only because Sulley cheated and rigged Mike's simulator settings! Mike is furious when he realises that his friend never believed he was scary in the first place.

Scare simulators were specially constructed in the amphitheatre – the site of the final event.

"You said you believed in me..."
— Mike

HOLLOW VICTORY

The truth is out when the rest of the OK gang overhear the row between Mike and Sulley. Their victory is a fake. Instead of celebrating triumph, Sulley is left alone and confused. He only wanted to help Mike, but now everything has gone wrong!

THE HUMAN WORLD

Upon learning that his winning scare was a fluke, Mike embarks on a daring mission into the human world to prove he has the skills to scare a real human child. However, all doesn't go as planned, as he ends up in a summer camp, surrounded by children in bunks. Just wait until the camp rangers turn up....

MIKE'S MISSION

Taking a key-card, Mike breaks into the Door Tech Lab and prepares to make an unauthorised trip out of his own world. He has to know once and for all whether he really is scary or not.

The curious kids at Camp Teamwork are not fazed by the little green guy in their midst. Could he be an alien?

FUNNY GUY

Mike's attempt at a scare has feeble results, as one of the kids thinks Mike is her cute imaginary friend, and tells him he looks funny!

TO THE RESCUE

Sulley realises with horror that his actions might have put Mike's life in danger. He rushes to the Door Tech Lab to rescue his friend – can the two finally put everything behind them and work together to get out of their sticky situation?

In moments, the whole cabin is awake. The late night commotion is sure to bring the rangers running.

HARDSCRABBLE'S HORROR

It takes a lot to frighten Dean Hardscrabble, but, for once, this is no simulation – and it is extremely dangerous. For this reason, she powers down the door leading to the cabin. The only way for Mike and Sulley to get back is to generate enough scream energy from their side of the door!

FRIGHTENING FRIENDSHIP

Mike and Sulley have a firm feeling about each other right from the start – extreme dislike! But somewhere along the way these two monsters realise they have more in common than they first thought....

First impression

"I knew Mike was impressed when we first met – right after I climbed through his window carrying a scare pig, and told him to shut up!"
— Sulley

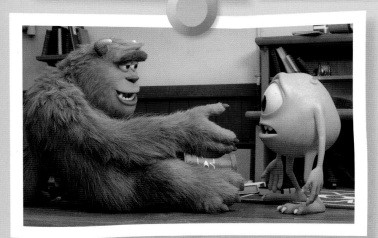

College rivals

"I had the big doofus pretty spooked from day one. He could see I was some kind of genius. I was determined to run circles round him. Maybe not literally."
— Mike

Special moments

"Good pals always have special memories to share. I'd say knocking over the dean's scream can was pretty memorable. But definitely not in a good way."
— Sulley

OK guys

"It was a big day when we both joined the OKs. I knew that winning the Scare Games was my last chance to make it back into the Scaring Programme – and I was sure that Sulley was going to ruin it all."

—Mike

A new start

"When Mike took us all to take a sneak peek at Monsters, Inc., I started to see what a great coach he was — and a pretty good guy too. We both realised we'd been idiots."

— Sulley

High five

"Big Blue has done some pretty dumb things in his time – but then I guess, so have I. One day I suddenly realised I had a friend for life. And now we're going places together!"

— Mike

THE END?

After being expelled and causing chaos by venturing into the human world, Mike and Sulley don't seem set for a happy ending. And yet, their incredible feat of scaring their way back into the Monster world made front page news. Will there be a final twist in their fortunes?

PARTING WORDS

Even Dean Hardscrabble is forced to change her mind about Mike and Sulley after all they have achieved. She can't let them stay at university, but admits they have done something no student ever did before – surprise her! Their parting is amicable as she wishes them good luck in the future.

The scare floors at Monsters, Inc. are always ready to welcome fresh talent….

"Wazowski and Sullivan are gonna change the world."
– Mike

"HELP WANTED"

There *is* a way into Monsters, Inc. without graduating from Monsters University – by getting a job in the post room! Starting at the bottom, the two pals will work their way up to janitors, café workers, scream-can wranglers – and finally to become the first scare team at Monsters, Inc. Together, Mike and Sulley are 100% scary!

It may not be quite how they planned it, but the two pals are happy to swap MU for Monsters, Inc.

ACKNOWLEDGEMENTS

LONDON, NEW YORK, MUNICH,
MELBOURNE and DELHI

Editor Emma Grange
Senior Editor Elizabeth Dowsett
Senior Designer Lynne Moulding
Senior Pre-Production Producer Jennifer Murray
Senior Producer Danielle Smith
Managing Editor Laura Gilbert
Design Manager Maxine Pedliham
Art Director Ron Stobbart
Publishing Manager Julie Ferris
Publishing Director Simon Beecroft

First published in Great Britain in 2013
by Dorling Kindersley Limited,
80 Strand, London, WC2R 0RL

10 9 8 7 6 5 4 3 2 1
001–187450–June/13

A CIP catalogue record for this book is
available from the British Library.

ISBN: 978-1-40933-037-0

Colour reproduction by Altaimage in the UK.
Printed and bound in Slovakia by TBB, a.s.

DK would like to thank Glenn Dakin for his writing.
DK would also like to thank John Tanzer, Chelsea Alon,
Shiho Tilley, Rima Simonian, Scott Tilley, Lori Tyminski,
Laura Uyeda and Winnie Ho at Disney Publishing.

Discover more at
www.dk.com
www.pixar.com

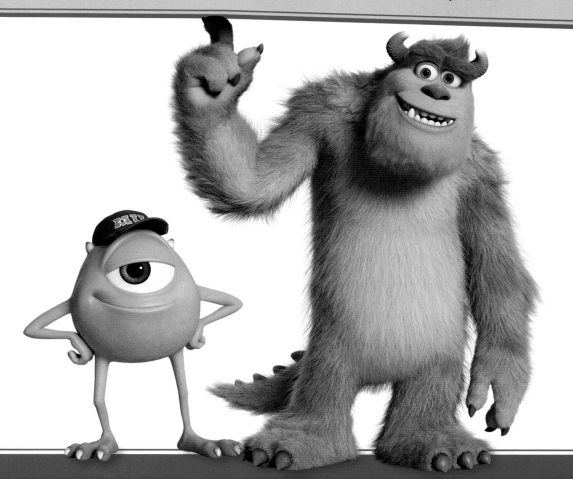